HARD TIMES:
POEMS OF ENCLOSURE

poems by

Bob A. Brown

Finishing Line Press
Georgetown, Kentucky

HARD TIMES:
POEMS OF ENCLOSURE

Copyright © 2021 by Bob A. Brown
ISBN 978-1-64662-601-4 First Edition
All rights reserved under International and Pan-American Copyright Conventions. No part of this book may be reproduced in any manner whatsoever without written permission from the publisher, except in the case of brief quotations embodied in critical articles and reviews.

ACKNOWLEDGMENTS

I thank my wife, Connie, for her unflagging encouragement and support. I am indebted to my mentors and editors Veronica Patterson and David Romtvedt, who encouraged and guided me. Thanks also to my writing group: Bill Hunter, Mary Kay Knief, Mary LaDouceur, Sandy McGarry, and Celia Turner, who gave me ideas about the early drafts of these poems. And I thank Father Paul Patin, S.J., for his friendship and support.

Publisher: Leah Huete de Maines
Editor: Christen Kincaid
Cover Art: B.A. Brown
Author Photo: Betsy Fecteau
Cover Design: Elizabeth Maines McCleavy

Order online: www.finishinglinepress.com
also available on amazon.com

Author inquiries and mail orders:
Finishing Line Press
PO Box 1626
Georgetown, Kentucky 40324
USA

Table of Contents

Foreword xi

Rush 1

Locked 2

Yearn 4

Choice 5

Saying Yes 6

Weather 8

Stranger 11

My Life 13

Half Way 14

Damage 15

Tattoo 16

Who Cares 17

Fuck Love 18

Hope 19

His Time 21

Landscape 22

Family 23

Mania 25

Unexpected 26

Good-Bye 27

Afterword 28

for Connie

Foreword

The poems in this collection are my attempt to capture a few of my experiences listening to and talking with prisoners as they did their time. I chose only these few to write about, from encounters over almost fifteen years.

The poems are also my effort to thank them, and to bid them goodbye.

Rush

A man rushes in.
"Please pray for my wife.
She's an addict and
disappeared. I'm
being released tonight
and must find her
before she kills herself."

He rushes out.

Locked

Called by a guard, the inmate
came in from a concrete yard
where, in rare sunshine, many
spend their one-hour respites.

He tapped his chest
and began a tale
of years spent
with a black hole for a soul.

Then he met a woman,
fell in love, married.
Her young daughter
called him Daddy.

For eight years he lived clean
and sober, grateful
for the gift of family.

His wife left him,
took the daughter.

Undone, he returned
to life on the street.

He asked for a priest—
to make his confession,
receive absolution.
No priest here. But

I told him God was always
with him—even
in that dark place—
that new life
could blossom in him.

Suddenly the jail
locked down. A guard
took him. Also locked down,
I prayed for him.

Yearn

Twenty-seven.
An enforcer for drug dealers.

Each week for months,
waiting for a plea.

Sentenced—
sixteen years—
we meet
a last time.

He tells how he and his girlfriend
took one debtor hostage. Enraged
by a report this man
had raped a seven-year-old girl,
they beat him. He
sodomized the man.
With ransom for the debt
promised for morning,
they waited, shooting meth.
Daybreak brought the police.

In prison he joined classes,
groups. Now
he yearns, he says,
for God.

He's never killed, but
he tells me
he always wanted to,
no one in particular.
Wistful,
no one in particular.

Choice
> *...he is the expiation for our sins...*
> —1 John 2:2

A prisoner asks
that we read 1 John 2:2,
a Bible verse his cellmate
suggested.

When I invite him
to read the verse aloud,
he stumbles on the words.
Slowly,
we sound out each word
until we come to
expiation. He asks what it means.

Puzzled, I finally offer,
"Christ's choice to die
on the cross, how his sacrifice
frees each of us from our guilt."

He's quiet.

Saying Yes

17, high on drugs, paranoid,
he shot and killed a man.

Now, after years of hard time
he may be released.

Once he worshipped
Satan, now asks if God
can forgive him.

I answer
with a dream
another convict told me:

> After a long journey
> of accidents, wrecks,
> an old man, wounded,
> I come to a house, enter.
>
> In the attic,
> I find a large chest,
> too heavy to move.
> I open it, find it full of muddy
> river rocks. One by one
> I remove them. Each
> is a violent memory.
>
> Beneath the rocks
> lies an ancient scroll, bound
> with glowing blue ribbons,
> sealed with red wax

I remove the ribbons,
break the seal, unroll
the scroll to find,
in meticulous script:

you are more than what
you think you are.
I love you,
Jesus."

The prisoner asks if this is true.
"Yes," I say

Weather

1. First meeting: storm clouds.

In a brightly lit locked room
we sat facing one another, on small
plastic chairs, a damaged
laminate-topped table between us.

A note from the chaplain
said the prisoner wanted
to talk with a Catholic.

He seemed surprised
by my visit, suspicious, as if
I was a law enforcement plant.

Lips compressed, he appeared
to be angry, but spoke
so fast and softly I had to ask
him to speak louder.

He said nothing about his life,
only told me about
sentences he had served
in jails and prisons.

When our time was up
I told him I would see him
again. He was silent.
I didn't like him.

2. Second meeting: clearing?

This time, a smile.
He asked how I was. When
I told him I had been ill,
he expressed concern.

He said he was OK,
had met that morning
with his public defender, argued
with her, threatened
to fire her for doing nothing
to obtain corroboration from
witnesses that he was not
at the scene of the crime.

Though he spoke up, I still
struggled to understand
his rapid speech.
He frequently laughed.

Infectiously. I laughed with him.
He said he needed
to be back at his job in the oil fields
to pay child support. When

we prayed, he prayed for
my safety and wellbeing,
crossed himself as he said
"Amen".

3. Third meeting: blue skies.

His anger is gone. He had fired
his public defender, now had
a private attorney. She had
followed through with depositions

from the witnesses.
He expects the charges
to be dropped the next day.
Together, we regard

the unpredictable nature of judges.
When I ask about his faith,
he says he saw only hypocrisy in churches,
but has his own journey with God.

Stranger

A meth addict, black stubs
for teeth, uneasy in his chair,
arms and hands
constantly moving, he told
me how tough he was—
how he could take care
of himself, was never afraid—
told of his plan to serve God,
to be a minister
of the Gospel of Jesus Christ.

The second time
I met with him,
his court date approaching,
he seemed sure he wouldn't
be sentenced to prison,
would serve only
months in this jail.

The third time, subdued.
There was a woman
who stole from his mother—
how he'd planned
to kill her son
in front of her,
then kill her.

High, armed with a knife
for the child, a pistol
for the mother, he waited
in front of the grocery store
where she shopped.

A young man approached,
said that he had been
on the road with friends,
that suddenly knew
he needed to be
at the grocery store.

The driver of the car
turned around, drove back to town
to the exact store.

Saw the man waiting there,
knew he was the one.

The stranger convinced him
to hand over the knife, the pistol,
took him to a café, stayed with him.

My Life

I wasn't doing anything wrong,
bothering anyone, just
sitting on the sidewalk,
drinking a cold beer from
the six pack in my knapsack.

A police car stopped.
Officers said I was violating
the open container laws.
So here I am,
in an orange suit again.

Why can't people
leave me alone? Just like
my sister and brother, always
wanting me to stop drinking.
So what

if I've had five DUIs? They've
each had one. A.A. doesn't
interest me—I really don't
want to stop drinking,
I enjoy it.

A twelve-pack of beer
and a mission meal
each a day—just right for me.
What's the big deal?
It's *my* life.

Half Way

He's afraid, knows
he will fail,
unable to sustain
"doing good,"

will go back to drugs, alcohol,
self-hate—stop seeing
others who accept him.
He still hopes

to be sentenced
to a half-way house, not
prison. Is a half-way house
realistic? I don't ask him.

He tells me of his wife,
two daughters, his fear
that his wife, an addict, is
running up debts they can't
pay. Nothing
about the children. Suddenly

he asks me to pray
for his cellie, in a wheelchair.
His cellie has told him
he'll never be able
to like himself until he stops
taking care of others,
not himself. Our time is up.

I pray for him,
his children, his wife, his cellie—
and for me,
for what I can bring—

Damage

Jailed for domestic abuse,
tells of wives, girlfriends,
partners responsible—
maybe even God.

Would he hold
hail-damaged roses
responsible for
their absence of scent,
the petals
strewn on the ground?

He explains himself,
justifies his anger,
refutes the undeserved
testimony against him.

If the bare roses lived,
he would forgive them—
expect blossoms.

I read to him from Job,
can no longer listen.

Tattoo

Weeping, the young man
says he wants out—
no more street life,
no more gang crime.

The frozen tear
by his eye tells
of murder,
danger, rivalry.

He knows
if word leaks
he'll be dead.
Frightened, asks

for help, advice,
prayers. The next time
I go to see him
I'm not allowed.

When I ask, the chaplain
looks away.

Who Cares?

A man
facing hard time, his
girlfriend pregnant,
wonders why God
has allowed this.

I listen quietly.

He weeps,
says he wants
a different life.

I tell him God's love is
always present, with a plan
for him that only patience
can unfold.

He stops weeping,
looks up, asks,
"A God who cares?"

Fuck Love

He showed me tattoos
on the inside of his biceps:
FUCK on the right,

LOVE on the left.
Said now he regretted
their permanence.

Son of druggies,
addicted in his teens,
he never experienced love.

Now, clean and sober,
he wants a companion,
a steady job.

He joined
a prison group,
where he encountered a topic

he struggled to grasp:
empathy. We talked,
his arms on the table.

Fuck on the right,
Love on the left.

Hope

> *...there is hope for a tree,*
> *if it be cut down, that it will sprout again.*
> —Job 14:7

African-American, unusual
in this county jail. Another man
from the streets of ready needles,

waiting to be sentenced,
hard time coming. In his fifties, tall,
ducked through the door.

His glasses were lost
during his arrest
for carrying a weapon:
small pliers he used
to make jewelry to sell
on the street. Now he waits
for new glasses.

He had believed himself slow—
struggled in school, dropped out.
Now, wry humor softening the dyslexia,
articulate, well-read, had waited
for weeks to be issued glasses
so he could read again.

He wept, blamed himself
for his mother's recent death—
high the last time he saw her,
locked up for her funeral.

Once, he brought pictures
of his family: clean cut sister,
brother-in-law, professional
basketball player nephews.

Shame kept him from
efforts to help him. His hope:
to be independent, to not use others.

The last time I see him
he tells me he wants
to go back to the streets clean,
help other street people—users, addicts—
extend mercy to them.

But for now
this jail where we sit,
the prison
where he will be going—
he tries for patience, forbearance.

His Time

The county District Attorney
offered him a plea bargain:
no more county jail time, all other
conditions already met.
His lawyer advised acceptance.
Assured of a brief
hearing before a judge—
in and out on the same day—
he accepted the plea.

Out on bail, he went home
to the east coast, his wife,
two small children, an extended
supportive family. A journeyman,
he worked full time at his trade.

On his required court date,
a round trip ticket in his pocket,
his bond paid, he appeared
before the judge. The plea bargain
was ignored. He was sentenced
to ninety days in the county jail.

Shocked, betrayed,
he struggled to overcome
despair, confusion.
For ninety days

he took on
a kitchen job, classes,
Catholic services,
completed the sentence.
Did his time.

Landscape
> ....*I am allotted months of emptiness,*
> *and nights of misery are apportioned to me.*
> —*Job 7:3*

Twelve years old, reading Treasure Island,
he had been baby-sitting
his five year old brother,
but didn't notice him leave.
When he looked up, searched the house,
not there; searched the yard, the shadowed
hedges, not there. Walked down the hill
to the pond. There. Drowned.

He grew up and married,
had two sons, naming the oldest after
the dead brother. On this son's
twelfth birthday, he gave him a bike—
proudly watched him ride it down
the street. To be struck
by a car and killed.

A landscape he can't comprehend.

Family

I live with
some other guys
in that park
by the railroad tracks,
near the river. You know
where.

      We're a family.
      We're always talking
      about God and
      his grace—pray
      a lot, every day.
      We're living
      a Christ-like life:
      no home, no job.

I'm scratching, because
we found a perfect place
for our toilet—
a patch of beautiful
red-leaved bushes.
Turned out to be
 poison sumac.

      Once, one of the guys,
      drunk, fell down, unconscious,
      pooped his pants.
      We took him to
      a homeless shelter,
      asked if we could
      clean him there.
      They refused.
      Aren't they Christians?
      We cleaned him
      in the river—so don't drink
      the river water!

Another time, we were out
of water. I took jugs
to the center, asked
to fill them. They refused.

I pushed by them,
through the door,
9*threw around
tables and chairs,

yelled at them. Then
I walked to a gas station,
filled the jugs there.

>Drinking's a problem,
>but I'm not ready to quit—
>I'd lose this family.

Thank you for coming.
Please come again—
pray for me,
and my family.

Mania

He introduces himself,
sits down, quickly
explains his arcane
cosmology, segues

to the ineffective medication
the medical staff
has given him—
not what he took before
to control his mania.
His hands jerk and move.

Through our small room's window
he points into
the room with tables
where he spends his one
solitary hour each day,

tells me with a rush
how he climbs over them,
under them, leaps
between them—tries
to scale the room's high walls.

He is waiting
for transport to another
county, then another state—
faces felony charges
both places. Whew.

I like him, this frantic
young man.

Unexpected

Sixty years old,
accused of theft—a bicycle—
he is now in respite
from winter streets.

Wild uncombed hair,
always clean when we meet—
toothless slurred speech, his
medicated tongue slipping
over smiling lips, as if
its extension might
grant him peace.
His siblings, out of touch,
avoid him.

I struggle to understand,
think he says he will pray for me—
then he laughs.

Is he an unexpected
messenger?

He tells me of Salvation
Army beds, sometimes full—
how he always makes street
comfort for himself: a sleeping
bag he is proud of.

Good-Bye

He had been a Satanist,
he told me, but had
a Christian cellmate
and wanted to know
a god of mercy.

A teenage murderer
now 34, he began
to come each week
to the communion service.

He asked me to be his mentor,
to share my own sometimes
reluctant journey to God.
I asked him to write a note,
tell me why. It said

he wanted to understand
God's plan for him.
"If I am called to be a Christian,
then I want to be one
with grace and humility."

Through many meetings,
side by side,
we traveled into a country
not on any map.

The day before his release
I'm not allowed through the gate—
some form in my file misplaced.

Afterword

another man done gone,
another man done gone,
another man done gone
from the county farm,
another man done gone.

—Vera Hall, 1940
Alan Lomax recording

The poetry chapbook *Hard Times: Poems of Enclosure* contains some of **Bob A. Brown's** poems written based on fifteen years as a religious volunteer in state prisons and a county jail.

Bob had written occasional poetry since college, but committed himself to writing only after hearing Robert Bly read his translation of Antonio Machado's poem that begins: "The wind, one brilliant day, called/ to my soul with an aroma of jasmine". He has since had a number of poems published in journals, as well as a poetry chapbook.

Bob is a retired Wyoming cattle rancher, Humanities Scholar with the Wyoming Humanities Council, and Jungian psychotherapist. He holds degrees from Yale University and the University of Denver.

After a home in northern Colorado, and many years ranching on Wyoming prairies, he now lives in New Mexico with his wife and irascible rescue cat.

www.ingramcontent.com/pod-product-compliance
Lightning Source LLC
LaVergne TN
LVHW041506070426
835507LV00012B/1375